Amazing Like You

Amazing like You...
Beckie 🅑

Written and illustrated by **Beckie Plant**

For Molly, Aimee, Kathrin, Jake & Daniel

What is a strength? What makes me me?
Why do I have them? Do I have three?

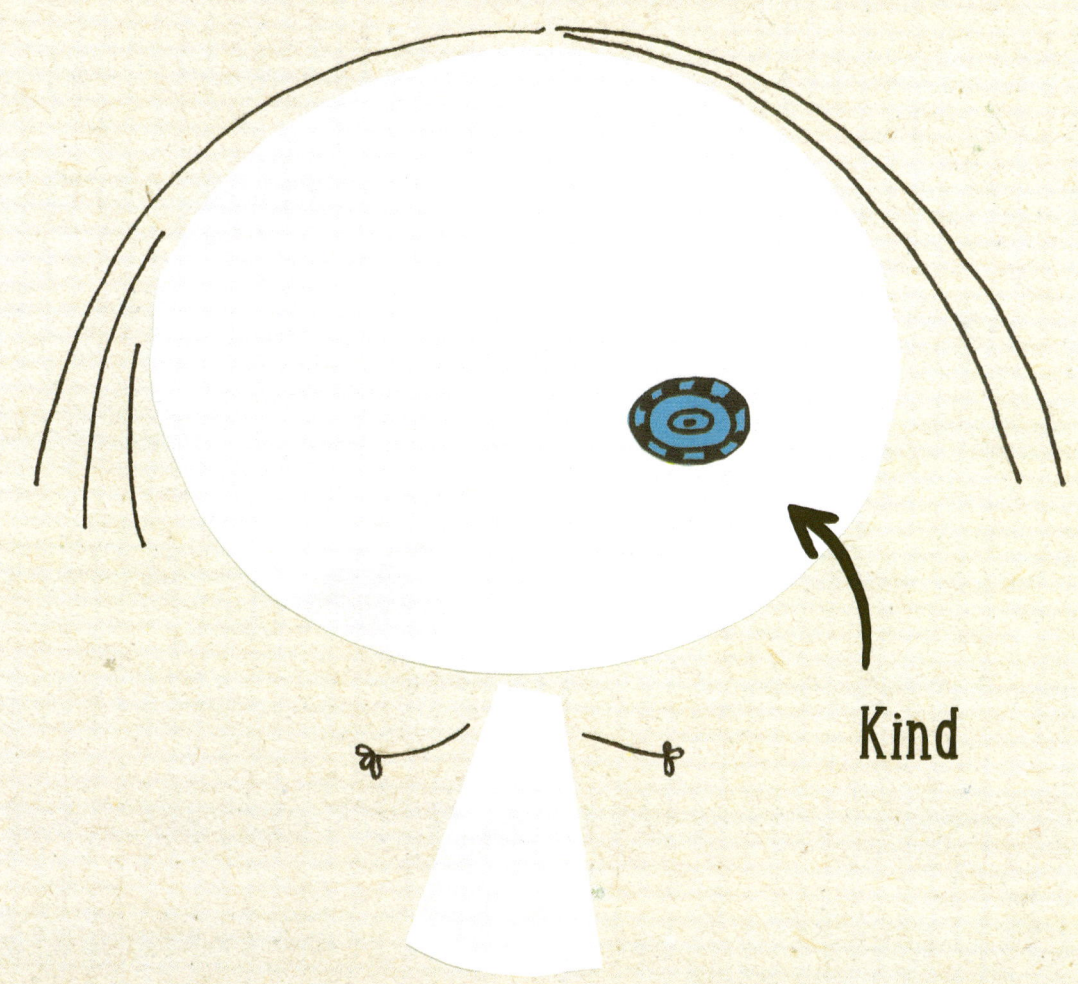

A strength is a power, deep deep in your mind,
one you're likely to have, is you like to be kind.

You say Please and Thank you, from morning to night,
a super strong magical strength, called polite.

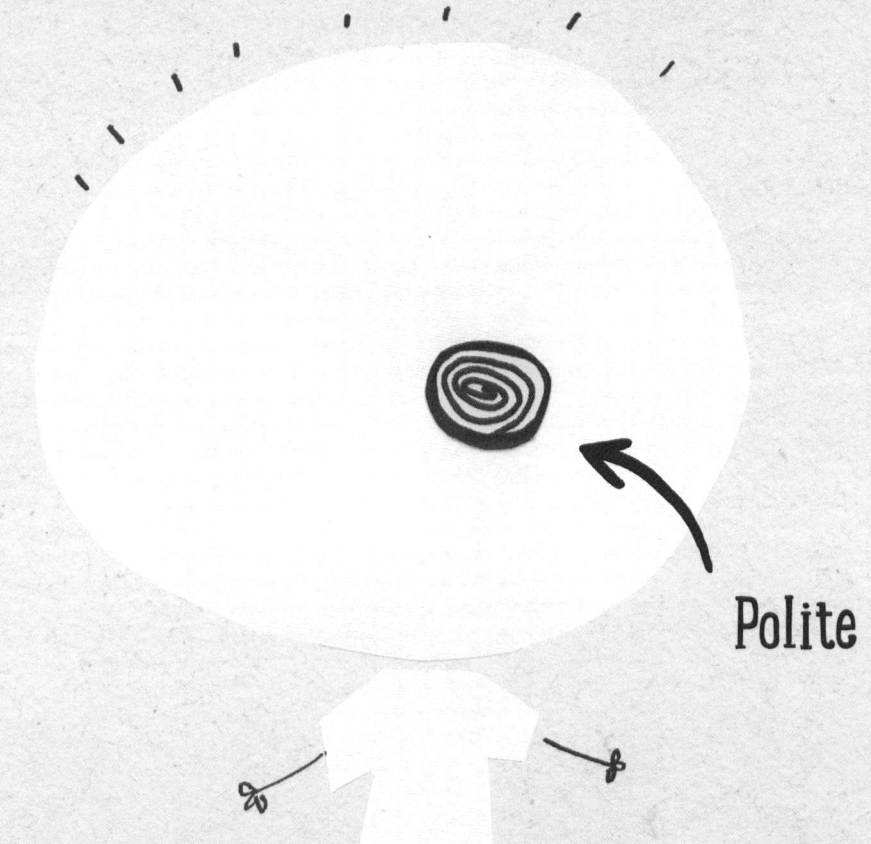

Polite

They are thoughts and emotions, we use at our best,
helping us to be happy and cope with the rest.

Think of these strengths, as balls in a pit,
taking up space, before no more will fit.

If all of these balls, are grumpy and sad,
we will be feeling, quite angry and mad.

We can try to fit in, a bright sunny thought,
but it bounces out, rolls away, can't be caught.

By throwing out bad thoughts, which say 'You cannot',
There is space for...

When we change our thinking, to balls which are strong,
our brain becomes a powerful, bright happy song.

You could make the balls, like fabulous flowers,
plant each positive thought, in a garden of powers.

Friend

You've not chased a lion, away round the bend,
but a strength you might be, is a very nice friend.

Sister

Brother

These powers you plant, as strengths you discover,
maybe you are, a great sister or brother.

Creative

Clever

Creative and clever, are things you might be,
it's building quite quickly, way more than three.

Cheerful   Happy

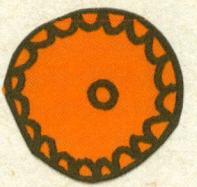  Beautiful smile

Are you cheerful and happy, with a beautiful smile?
If you are these things, I sure like your style.

Quiet

Gentle

Still

Do you sometimes be quiet, and gentle, and still?
So many great strengths in that garden you fill.

Brave

Strong

Caring

Forgiving

Patient

Are you brave, are you caring, forgiving or strong?
Can you sit and be patient when things take too long?

Helpful

Care

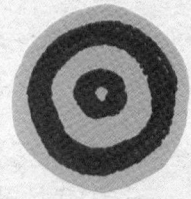
Fair

Are you helpful to others, and show that you care?
When playing a game, do you do what is fair?

Take care and show love, to the strengths in your thinking,
they will grow just as fast, as your eyes do a blinking.

You can choose anything, for these strengths to be, bright cheerful fish, in your own special sea.

If flowers and gardens, just isn't your look,
make a powerful library, each strength is a book.

Look after these powers, they make you amazing,
like stars in the sky, at night, when you're gazing.

There are so many strengths, You can choose who to be,

you have yours, you are you, I have mine, I am me.

Take deep breaths, and believe,
because it is true,
your strengths are unique
and...

Copyright © 2023 Beckie Plant

All rights reserved. No part of this publication may be reproduced, distributed, or transmitted in any form or by any means, including photocopying, recording, or other electronic or mechanical methods, without the prior written permission of the publisher, except in the case of brief quotations embodied in critical reviews and certain other noncommercial uses permitted by copyright law.

Beckie Plant (author and illustrator)

Amazing Like You

ISBN 978-1-922957-60-3

Childrens book

Cover and book design by Green Hill Publishing